A Suitable Helper

A Good Steward of God's Resources

Dena Crecy

Copyright © 2012 by Dena Crecy

A Suitable Helper
by Dena Crecy

Printed in the United States of America

ISBN 9781622300877

All rights reserved. No portion of this book may be reproduced, stored in a retrieval system, or transmitted in any form or by any means—electronic, mechanical, photocopy, recording, or any other—except for brief quotation in printed reviews, without the prior permission of the author. The views expressed in this book are not necessarily those of the publisher.

Scripture taken from the *Holy Bible*, New King James Version (NKJV), Copyright 1979, 1980, 1982 by Thomas Nelson, Inc. Used by permission. All rights reserved.

Scripture quotations marked NLT are taken from The Holy Bible, New Living Translation (NLT). Copyright © 1986 by the Tyndale House Publishers, Wheaton, Illinois, 60189. Used by permission. All rights reserved.

Scripture quotations marked MSG are taken from The Holy Bible, The Message Translation (MSG). Copyright © 1993, 1994, 1995, 1996, 2000, 2001, 2002 by Eugene H. Peterson. Used by permission. All rights reserved.

Four Spiritual Laws is an evangelistic Christian tract created in 1952 by Bill Bright, founder of Campus Crusade for Christ, the world's largest Christian Ministry. (It is what was used to bring me to Christ). Used by permission. All rights reserved.

www.xulonpress.com

DEDICATION

To my MOM, who loved me dearly until the day she died, October, 1987.

To my brother Gilbert, who was a wonderful brother until the day he died, March, 2005.

To my sister Tricia, who has a quiet strength and perseverance that I truly admire. As you continue to live cancer free, may you continue to believe that God does love you and has a wonderful plan for your life.

To my oldest brother Arthur, may you know and embrace the love of God and the wonderful plan He has for your life.

To my wonderful children, Sean and Sydney, who loved me even though they got very tired of hearing the words, "It's not in the budget." OR "I did not plan for this item or activity." My prayer for you both is that you come to know God and allow HIM to be the center of your life and your finances.

To my darling grandson, Jaden, thank you for allowing me to be your Granny. Please know that I love you very much. Please, please, also know that God loves you and has a wonderful plan for your life, which includes your finances.

To a dear friend, Terri H. Thanks so much for all your encouragement and support with this project. Your willingness to assist with editing and provide valuable feedback allowed me to continue on. Too bad those twins came on August 13, 2012, before we had a chance to complete this project. However, I realize that completing this project was God's top priority for your life. Congratulations to you and Greg for bringing Samuel and Sophie into the world. Maybe they will read my book when they grow up.

ACKNOWLEDGMENTS

Vikki Wells, for the Proverbs31Marketing Ministry and the, "How to Write a Book/Screenplay in 30 Days" class and the students who took the class with me. It was a tremendous help to this project.

Donna Kozik – For the, "Write a Book in a Weekend" virtual class. It too, was a tremendous help to this project.

Stewardship Ministry of Oak Cliff Bible Fellowship who lead by example on how to manage resources God's way, according to God's word. Also, for your constant love, support and encouragement throughout this project.

Roz Warfield for bringing me the Dragon software and sending me texts and voice mails to push me through.

Ken Kilgore, who has taken the journey to true financial freedom with me, and has been a tremendous resource of encouragement and support.

Book Epigraph

There's a Deep Hole in My Sidewalk
    By Portia Nelson

Chapter I
I walk down the street.
There is a deep hole in the sidewalk
I fall in.
I am lost … I am helpless.
It isn't my fault.
It takes forever to find a way out.

Chapter II
I walk down the same street.
There is a deep hole in the sidewalk.
I pretend I don't see it.
I fall in again.
I can't believe I am in the same place.
But, it isn't my fault.

It still takes a long time to get out.

Chapter III
I walk down the same street.
There is a deep hole in the sidewalk.
I *see* it is there.
I still fall in … it's a habit … but,
my eyes are open.
I know where I am.
It is *my* fault.
I get out immediately.

Chapter IV
I walk down the same street.
There is a deep hole in the sidewalk.
I walk around it.

Chapter V
I walk down another street.

Which chapter best describes your financial life right now? What could you do to turn the page and start over? Whether you are Single or married, as you turn the pages in this book, you will discover God's order and plan for YOUR financial life. As you embrace the principles, you will discover, they will work with all the sidewalks in your life that have deep holes.

TABLE OF CONTENTS

Introduction xv
Call to Action 17
1. Recognize – There is a deep hole in your financial sidewalk 27
2. Release – What the world says about it. Blaming Others 34
3. Reflect – Accept responsibility for your financial decisions 44
4. Receive – Open your eyes. Know where you are. 48
5. Retain – Walk around the deep hole. 63
6. Rejoice – As you walk down another street. 92
7. Revisit/Review – "Good planning and hard work lead to prosperity……" Proverbs 21:5 98
8. A Suitable Helper – A Good Steward of God's Resources 103
9. Resource Page 111

INTRODUCTION

Ladies, let me start off by saying that this is not a "Get Rich Quick" book or a prosperity message. It is about taking God seriously in the management or stewardship of the resources that He has provided.

The poem that you just read by Portia Nelson called, "There's a Hole in My sidewalk", is about change, or the need for it, to get the desired results in our lives. In this case, it is our financial life. We will use this poem and many passages from the Bible as we travel together on this journey.

Many of us have heard, and may have even said it once or twice ourselves, the statement, "The definition of insanity is doing the same thing over and over and expecting different results." We say it to people. We laugh and joke about it; however, if we take a close look at our lives, we will discover that this statement is true in many areas of our lives. Don't worry!

In this book, we are only going to focus on one area, the financial area.

I began this financial freedom journey in 2005 and it has totally changed my life. While travelling on this journey, God has allowed me to **recognize** some things, **release** some things, **reflect** on some things, **receive** some things, **retain** those things and **rejoice** as I have experienced more of God in my financial life.

Please come on the journey with me in the following pages of this book.

Passage Matthew 6:19-21:

Teaching about Money and Possessions

[19] "Don't store up treasures here on earth, where moths eat them and rust destroys them, and where thieves break in and steal. [20] Store your treasures in heaven, where moths and rust cannot destroy, and thieves do not break in and steal. [21] Wherever your treasure is, there the desires of your heart will also be. (NLT)

Call to Action:

In order to receive and embrace the principles in this book, there is a pre-requisite; you must have a relationship with Jesus Christ.

Knowing God Personally
Find God - What does it take to know God? This will explain how you can personally begin a relationship with God, right now.

What does it take to begin a relationship with God? Wait for lightning to strike? Devote yourself to unselfish religious deeds? Become a better person so that God will accept you? NONE of these. God has made it very clear in the Bible how we can know Him. This will explain how you can personally begin a relationship with God, right now...

Principle One: God loves you and offers a wonderful plan for your life.

God created you. Not only that, He loves you so much that He wants you to know Him now and spend eternity with Him. Jesus said, "For God so loved the world that He gave His only Son so that everyone who believes in Him will not perish but have eternal life." *John 3:16*

Jesus came so that each of us could know and understand God in a personal way. Jesus alone can bring meaning and purpose to life.

What keeps us from knowing God? ...

Principle Two: All of us sin and our sin has separated us from God.

We sense that separation, that distance from God because of our sin. The Bible tells us that "All of us like sheep have gone astray; each of us has turned to his own way." *Isaiah 53:6*

Deep down, our attitude may be one of active rebellion or passive indifference toward God and His ways, but it's all evidence of what the Bible calls sin.

The result of sin in our lives is death—spiritual separation from God. *Romans 6:23* Although we may try to get close to God through our own effort, we inevitably fail.

The diagram below shows the great gap that exists between us and God. The arrows illustrate how we might try to reach God through our own efforts. We may try to do good things in life, or earn God's acceptance through a good life or a moral philosophy. But our good efforts are insufficient to cover up our sin.

How can we bridge this gulf?...

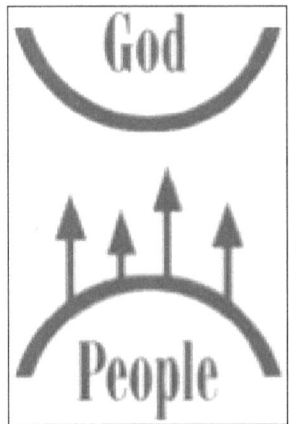

Principle Three: Jesus Christ is God's only provision for our sin. Through Him we can know and experience God's love and plan for our life.

We deserve to pay for our own sin. The problem is, the payment is death. So that we would not have to die separated from God, out of his love for us, Jesus Christ died in our place.

The Bible states that Jesus is "the image of the invisible God...by Him all things were created..." *Colossians 1:15,16* Jesus was crucified for blasphemy—for clearly identifying himself as equal to God—which He was.

On the cross, Jesus took all of our sin on Himself and completely, fully paid for it. "For Christ also died for sins...the just for the unjust, so that He might bring us to God." *I Peter 3:18* "...He saved us, not because of righteous things we had done, but because of His mercy." *Titus 3:5* Because of Jesus' death on the cross, our sin doesn't have to separate us from God any longer.

"For God so loved the world that He gave His only Son, so that everyone who believes in Him will not perish but have eternal life." *John 3:16*

Jesus not only died for our sin, He rose from the dead. *I Corinthians 15:3-6* When He did, He proved beyond a doubt that He can rightfully promise eternal life—that He is the Son of God and the only means by which we can know God. That is why Jesus said, "I am the way, the truth and the life; no one can come to the Father except through me." *John 14:6*

Instead of trying harder to reach God, He tells us how we can begin a relationship with Him right now. Jesus says, "Come to me." "If anyone thirsts, let him come to me and drink. Whoever believes in me… out of his heart will flow rivers of living water." *John 7:37,38* It was Jesus' love for us that caused Him to endure the cross. And He now invites us to come to Him, that we might begin a personal relationship with God.

Just knowing what Jesus has done for us and what he is offering us is not enough. To have a relationship with God, we need to welcome Him into our life…

Principle Four: We must individually accept Jesus Christ as Savior and Lord.

The Bible says, "Yet to all who received Him, to those who believed in His name, He gave the right to become children of God." *John 1:2*

We accept Jesus by faith. The Bible says, "God saved you by His special favor when you believed. And you can't take credit for this; it is a gift from God. Salvation is not a reward for the good things we have done, so none of us can boast about it." *Ephesians 2:8,9*

Accepting Jesus means believing that Jesus is the Son of God, who He claimed to be, then inviting Him to guide and direct our lives. *John 3:1-8* Jesus said, "I came that you might have life, and have it more abundantly." *John 10:10*

And here is Jesus' invitation. He said, "I'm standing at the door and I'm knocking. If anyone hears my voice and opens the door, I will come in." *Revelation 3:20*

How will you respond to God's invitation? Consider these two circles:

 **Self-Directed Life**	ˢSelf is on the throne †Jesus is outside the life •Decisions and actions are solely directed by self, often resulting in frustration
 **Christ-Directed Life**	†Jesus is in the life and on the throne ˢSelf is yielding to Jesus •The person sees Jesus' influence and direction in their life

Which circle best represents your life?

Which circle would you like to have represent your life?

Begin a relationship with Jesus…

You can receive Christ right now. Remember that Jesus says, "I'm standing at the door and I'm knocking. If anyone hears my voice and opens the door, I will come in." *Revelation 3:20* Would you like to respond to His invitation? Here's how.

The precise words you use to commit yourself to God are not important. He knows the intentions of your heart. If you are unsure of what to pray, this might help you put it into words:

"Jesus, I want to know you. I want you to come into my life. Thank you for dying on the cross for my sin so that I could be fully accepted by you. Only you can give me the power to change and become the person you created me to be. Thank you for forgiving me and giving me eternal life with God. I give my life to you. Please do with it as you wish. Amen."

If you sincerely asked Jesus into your life just now, then He has come into your life as He promised. You have begun a personal relationship with God.

What follows is a lifelong journey of change and growth as you get to know God better through Bible reading, prayer and interaction with other Christians.

If you just made a decision for Christ, please email me at relationshipsgodstyle@yahoo.com and you will receive a special gift.

If you need questions answered before you can make a decision for Christ, please email your questions to <u>relationshipsgodstyle@yahoo.com</u>.

1

Recognize – There's a deep hole in my financial sidewalk.

¹¹ Yours, O LORD, is the greatness, the power, the glory, the victory, and the majesty. Everything in the heavens and on earth is yours, O LORD, and this is your kingdom. We adore you as the one who is over all things. ¹² Wealth and honor come from you alone, for you rule over everything. Power and might are in your hand, and at your discretion people are made great and given strength.
1 Chronicles 29:11-12:

The previous passage of scripture is the 2nd of 10 verses that we have to memorize in the Crown Financial Life Group class. Those verses literally changed my financial life! I never thought about the fact that God owns everything, yes, everything! Because I did not recognize it, there was a deep hole in my financial sidewalk.

When I signed up for the class, I had no idea what I was signing up for. I accepted in Christ in 1984, in a strong Bible teaching church in Houston, Texas. I learned, believed and practiced the 10 percent tithing principle, and was glad to do it! I was taught to give 10 percent of my gross income, and, "the first fruits of ALL my increase, as well as an offering.

9Honour the LORD with thy substance, and with the first fruits of all thine increase:

10So shall thy barns be filled with plenty, and thy presses shall burst out with new wine.

Proverbs 3:9-10

However, what I did recognize was the fact that I needed to consult God on the remaining 90 percent, because it all belongs to HIM. Whatever I thought I owned was not really mine, I am just a steward.

This concept was brought to light when we were asked to raise our hands if we owned something. Most of us raised our hands, because we owned something, or so we thought. We were then informed of Colossians 1:16, which states………

"16 for through him God created everything in the heavenly realms and on earth. He made the things we can see and the things we can't see—such as thrones, kingdoms, rulers, and authorities in the unseen world.

Everything was created through HIM and for HIM.

After coming to the realization, or recognizing, that we owned nothing, all things were created by HIM and for HIM, we then discovered that we were in financial bondage.

What is financial bondage? Financial bondage is the state of feeling overwhelmed, stressed out, like your drowning, beat down, etc, by matters of money. You feel like your money has you captured and won't let you go!

Symptoms of Financial Bondage:
- Get rich quick attitude – Proverbs 28:22 *"22 Greedy people try to get rich quick but don't realize they're headed for poverty.*
- Overdue bills
- Making minimum payments
- Cash advance on one card to pay another
- Payday loans
- Paying late every month (it is a habit)
- Conflicts in relationships – Hebrews 12:15, *"15 Look after each other so that none of you fails to receive the grace of God. Watch out that no poisonous root of bitterness grows up to trouble you, corrupting many."*

Do you have any of the above symptoms? I know I did. I pretty much had all of them at one time or another. I was always looking for some get rich quick opportunity. I sold Avon, Tupperware, Mary Kay, Primerica Products and Jewelry. None of them turned out to be the plan God had for MY life.

I had overdue bills, and the bills I could pay, I paid late. I did not have credit cards, because my credit would not allow me to get them. THANK GOD! However, I did indulge in payday loans. The email offers were coming right and left and I buckled under the pressure and temptation. Once I recognized my responsibility and faced it, I was able to work out payment arrangements and clear them up.

As a single parent (divorced), I took my financial stress out on my children. They would tell me I was grouchy sometimes and I just brushed it off. I had no idea that what I was feeling, or even expressing to them was tied to the frustrations and failure I was feeling regarding my financial life.

The class helped me recognize that God's will for my financial life, and my whole life for that matter, is financial peace. Shalom – peace on all sides, including financial peace.

[27] *"I am leaving you with a gift—peace of mind and heart. And the peace I give is a gift the world cannot give. So don't be troubled or afraid.* John 14:27

[7] *Then you will experience God's peace, which exceeds anything we can understand. His peace will guard your hearts and minds as you live in Christ Jesus."* Philippians 4:7

God's will is peace *in* the storm, not absence of storms – John 16:33

³³ I have told you all this so that you may have peace in me. Here on earth you will have many trials and sorrows. But take heart, because I have overcome the world."

The same process that we used to recognize the need for a savior and accept Jesus Christ as that savior, is the same process we must go through as we recognize the need for help with managing our financial life. The first step of the 12 step Alcoholics Anonymous program puts it like this:

1. We admitted we were powerless over alcohol—that our lives had become unmanageable.

We can rewrite it to say that we admit or recognize that we are powerless over money—that our financial lives had become unmanageable.

Questions to Ponder:
1. Have you recognized that you don't own anything and that God owns everything?

2. Have you recognized and/or admitted that you are in financial bondage?
3. Have you recognized and/or accepted God's will of financial peace for your life?

2

Release – What the world says about the matter.
Blaming Others

Romans 12
A Living Sacrifice to God

¹ And so, dear brothers and sisters, I plead with you to give your bodies to God because of all he has done for you. Let them be a living and holy sacrifice— the kind he will find acceptable. This is truly the way to worship him. ² Don't copy the behavior and customs of this world, **but let God transform you into a new person by changing the way you think. Then you will learn to know God's will for you, which is good and pleasing and perfect.**

Alcoholic Anonymous (AA) steps 2 & 3

2. Came to believe that a Power greater than ourselves could restore us to sanity.
3. Made a decision to turn our (*financial*) will and our (*financial*) lives over to the care of God *as we understood Him.*

Recognizing I needed to do something different as it relates to my finances was the easy part for me. I just did not make the connection that in order to do something different, I had to change the way I viewed money, finances and wealth. Recognizing was not enough. If I wanted a different or better result, I had to do some things differently.

In order to receive this new information, I had to make room for it by getting rid of my present view of money, finances and wealth. In our financial freedom class, we are taught to "lay aside the weight" or throw off everything that hinders", as it stated in Hebrews 12:1...

[1] Therefore, since we are surrounded by such a huge crowd of witnesses to the life of faith, let us strip off every weight that slows us down, especially the sin

that so easily trips us up. And let us run with endurance the race God has set before us.

For me, I had to release the voices in my head that did not match God's word. Release the beliefs that I had come to embrace that did not match God's word. Pretty much, I had to release everything that I had come to know was truth and right that did not line up with the word of God. This was very hard to do because the norm is to listen to people's opinions, and and believe the world's view because it appears to be right. Watching television, talking to people at work, and even talking to people at church became really hard, when the conversation did not match the word of God. However, if I really wanted the financial change that I said I wanted, I had to release the old and embrace the new. This was just one of the drastic changes the class talked about.

There were also some other things that I had to release.

    a. Hasty decisions (operating without a plan) Proverbs 21:5

    b. View of credit card spending & carrying long term balances

    c. Buy now and pay later mind set

d. "I got to have it" or "I deserve it" attitude
e. Blaming my mother and my up bringing (*my mother and grandmother were broke and did not know how to handle money and therefore, did not teach me*)
f. Blaming a generation curse (*my mother and grandmother were broke single parents, so that must be my lot in life*)
g. Blaming my husband. He left me with 2 small children and he handled the finances in our household. It is all his fault.
h. Pride – Confess to God that I have not handled HIS money HIS way or according to the plan HE has for MY life. (*my thoughts vs. HIS thoughts – Isaiah 55:8*)

I had to release all of the above and stop blaming people and situations for the bad financial decisions I made. It was my fault and I had to make a decision to do something about it. I did the last item first; I swallowed my pride and confessed to God that I have not handled HIS money HIS way, and received HIS forgiveness, as stated in 1 John 1:9....

⁹ But if we confess our sins to him, he is faithful and just to forgive us our sins and to cleanse us from all wickedness.

One thing that helped me to release was to move out of my townhome when my lease was up in the summer of 2005. I gave away all of mine and my children's things to a friend and his mother. They took everything except a few clothes that we carried with us. I mean everything! Furniture, pictures, dishes, linen, bathroom things, everything.

The Lord moved us into the Budget Suites of America. It is an extended stay hotel. It is a fully furnished, one bedroom apartment with all utilities paid, including cable and internet. The monthly fee was actually cheaper than my townhome, utilities, phone and cable. We did not have internet before, so that was a bonus. The kitchen was furnished with dishes, pots/pans, and silverware and cooking utensils. I was very excited about the financial journey I was traveling on. Of course, my kids were not happy. They were teenagers (19 & 14) and could not invite their friends over to such a place. Well, of course, this made me *very* happy, as I did not want the company anyway.

With the move, I was able to shed quite a bit of stuff that I was hanging on to for the sake of hanging on to. The class brought up a question, "If you passed away today, what would your family do with all the things you have been keeping?" WOW! That question really got me to thinking. What would my family do with all the stuff I had been saving and storing anyway? My Pastor, Tony Evans, informed us that America is the only country in the world that pays for storage. He says if you have not touched it or used in six months, get rid of it. Don't pay for storage. I heard and received that right away. Every six months I continue to release what I do not use or need. We should make three piles as we release, a keep pile, a trash pile and a donate pile. I only keep things I believe my children will want as a memory of me. All of the pictures that I had in plastic storage containers that did not have me in them, or they did not know the people, I shredded them, as that is what they will do after I am gone. Little things that I had been saving for who knows what, I either gave away or donated if my children did not want.

I also had to release some people and activities. This was a very humbling process. At the time of my move, I was very active in our Singles' Ministry as a small group facilitator, and was holding the meetings in my home. It appeared to be hard for the ladies to come to the meetings at the hotel. I knew I was not going to move any time soon, so I gave up the group. My focus was on God and HIS plan for my life and not peoples' comfort level.

One of the other things that was called out was to notice what we were putting in our heads and release what does not line up with the Word of God. What type of money discussions were we having with friends and coworkers? If we were always talking about how broke we were and how hard things were, we needed to change our conversation, as that was not going to help us stay focused, and it did not match what God was saying about HIS plan for our life. What are we listening to? Radio? Television? What are we reading? Does it match up with the word of God? Sound extreme? Well, it is! We have to make a decision to live every part of our life according to the word of God. We must do this and not apologize for it. We must make a drastic change in our lives to get the desire that we want for our money. We have to believe that God loves us and has a wonderful plan for our life.

¹¹ For I know the plans I have for you," says the LORD. "They are plans for good and not for disaster, to give you a future and a hope. Jeremiah 29:11

Before the class, my mindset was making hasty financial decisions, as I was not living on a budget. I did not have a set plan for my spending. I thought "by now, pay later" was the way to go. However, in the class, I learned that layaway was a plan from God. I also thought I had to have it or I deserved it. I used to tell my ex-husband that all the time. When we were married was the only time I actually lived on a budget. He was an excellent financial planner, and he really knew how to save money. I had never lived on a budget before, so after we got married, I would tell him all the time that he could not tell me when to spend or how much to spend. After all, I worked just liked he did and he could not tell me how to spend my money. After I accepted Christ and learned how to submit, I changed my mindset about it. Especially, after going to the class, I learned that the, "I got to have it now", or "I deserve it now" mindset brought me financial suffering later, that did not feel good.

Now I know some of you have lots of things that you believe you just cannot get rid of. You may have them neatly packed into boxes or those nice plastic containers from the container store. Some of you cannot even park in your garage because it is full of stuff. Ladies, I know there are clothes, shoes, etc, in your closet and chest of drawers that you have never worn. And, I bet the price tag is still attached. What are you doing with all that stuff? Are there things that you have not looked at or touched for six months or more? If so, get rid of it! Free yourself! This is part of being a good steward of God's resources. Someone could use the stuff you are just holding on to. Think about it. Pray about it. God may lead you to have a garage sale to make some money to pay off some debt. Or, HE may ask you to give it away to your church or another charitable organization. HE does want you to be free. This is something you can do right now, and it will not cost you anything, but some time.

As I stated earlier, releasing is the hardest pill to swallow. It involves making a drastic change in your thinking, which will result in a drastic change in your financial life. Stop pretending you don't see the deep hole in your sidewalk. Stop blaming people or circumstances. It does not have to take a long time to get out. Let's review.

I walk down the same street.

There is a deep hole in the sidewalk.

I pretend I don't see it.

I fall in again.

I can't believe I am in the same place.

But, it isn't my fault.

It still takes a long time to get out.

Questions to Ponder:
1. What do you need to see?
2. What do you need to move away from?
3. What habits do you need to change?
4. Who are you blaming?
5. What circumstances or situations are you holding on to?
6. What do YOU need to confess and surrender to God?
7. What do YOU need to release?

3

Reflect – Accept responsibility for YOUR financial decisions.

Isaiah 55:8:

[8] *"My thoughts are nothing like your thoughts,"*
says the LORD.
"And my ways are far beyond anything
you could imagine.

AA Steps 4 & 5
4. Made a searching and fearless moral inventory of ourselves.
5. Admitted to God, to ourselves, and to another human being the exact nature of our wrongs.

Now that you have connected with Christ regarding your finances and released all of the stuff that did not line up with HIS word, it is time to reflect on financial decisions that we have made that we are still suffering from. We have confessed them and we will not dwell on them; however, we do want to know what was going on inside our heads at the time we made those decisions.

We have just read Isaiah 55:8, and now understand that His thoughts are not our thoughts and His ways are not our ways. When we truly believe that statement, we will learn not to make any more bad financial decisions.

Finance is a very sensitive subject and we generally do not like to get other people involved. The problem with that is it goes against what the Bible says. There are many scriptures that mention getting wise counsel. One that we had to memorize in the class is Proverbs 12:15, *"15 Fools think their own way is right, but the wise listen to others.*

When I read that verse, I knew that the Bible was telling me I was a fool regarding my finances, as I thought my own way was right. God brought back to my remembrance the times I had made financial decisions without consulting HIM, without having a plan, and without getting wise counsel. OUCH! Very painful! I do not want to live like that again. The key is wise counsel, not just counsel.

How do you seek wise counsel? The Bible tells us how.

Psalm 1:1 - *Oh, the joys of those who do not follow the advice of the wicked, or stand around with sinners, or join in with mockers.*

Proverbs 1:15 - *Let the wise listen to these proverbs and become even wiser. Let those with understanding receive guidance*

Proverbs 11-15 - *Without good direction, people lose their way; the more wise counsel you follow, the better your chances. (MSG)*

Proverbs 15:22 - *Refuse good advice and watch your plans fail; take good counsel and watch them succeed.(MSG)*

Proverbs 19:20 - *Get all the advice and instruction you can, so you will be wise the rest of your life.*

These are just a few verses on the importance of wise counsel. As we seek wise counsel we need to make sure that we pray about the counsel we receive. The Holy Spirit will confirm what we should receive and what we should discard. Remember, wise counsel is seeking counsel from experts in the area. Of course, we should seek out counsel from people who are walking with God and believe as we believe, but it is not an absolute. We just need to bathe all decisions in prayer, before we make a decision.

Questions to Ponder:
1. What financial decisions have I made that required wise counsel?
2. Who can I ask to be my accountability partner? Who will ask me the hard questions about my financial decision before I make it?
3. If there is not one currently, ask God to provide one for you and HE will.

4

Receive – Open Your Eyes. Know Where You Are.

Chapter III
I walk down the same street.
There is a deep hole in the sidewalk.
I *see* it is there.
I still fall in … it's a habit … but,
<u>my eyes are open.</u>
<u>I know where I am.</u>
<u>It is *my* fault.</u>
<u>I get out immediately.</u>

I pray that your heart will be flooded with light so that you can understand the confident hope he has given to those he called—his holy people who are his rich and glorious inheritance.
Ephesians 1:18

AA Steps 6 & 7

> *6. Were entirely ready to have God remove all these defects of character.*
>
> *7. Humbly asked Him to remove our shortcomings.*

Let's review. We have recognized where we have gone astray. We have confessed our sins. We have reflected on our decision making process, and we understand the importance of wise counsel. It is now time to receive all that God has for us by way of our finances.

First, we have to receive the fact that God is a God of order, and HE has an order for our finances. I have heard many Pastors and Bible Teachers teach on this subject, and they have a common theme: Give, Save, Spend (*with a written plan*) and learn Contentment. Once we receive these facts, they will radically change our financial life, it definitely changed mine!

Give – Establish the Tithe

Most of us who grew up in church have heard more than one version of how to give to God. What I have found to be true is what the Bible says about giving. We should give one tenth of all that we receive for the advancement of God's work, AND we should do it cheerfully.

⁹You are cursed with the curse, for you are robbing Me, even this whole nation. ¹⁰Bring all the tithes (the whole tenth of your income) into the storehouse, that there may be food in My house, and prove Me now by it, says the Lord of hosts, if I will not open the windows of heaven for you and pour you out a blessing, that there shall not be room enough to receive it. ¹¹And I will rebuke the devourer [insects and plagues] for your sakes and he shall not destroy the fruits of your ground, neither shall your vine drop its fruit before the time in the field, says the Lord of hosts. Malachi 3:9-11

³⁸ Give, and you will receive. Your gift will return to you in full—pressed down, shaken together to make room for more, running over, and poured into your lap. The amount you give will determine the amount you get back. Luke 6:38

⁶ Remember this—a farmer who plants only a few seeds will get a small crop. But the one who plants generously will get a generous crop. ⁷ You must each decide in your heart how much to give. And don't give reluctantly or in response to pressure. "For God loves a person who gives cheerfully.". 2 Corinthians 9:6-7

Tithing is the most important part of giving. You have to believe that all of the Bible is true, and not just parts of it. Tithing is at least a tenth of all you receive, and it is the first tenth of all you receive. Now, I know what you are thinking, 'do I give off of my gross or my net income?' What I believe is if God is first in our financial lives, our giving will reflect that. Think about it, if taxes can be taken off of the gross of what you receive, why would you give to God off of the net? We have to believe that the above verses are true. Malachi 3, verse 10, challenges us to "prove me now". I have chosen to believe the word, and it has always proven true for me. Even when it seems like I did not have enough, I did what I had purposed in my heart, to bring the whole tithe to the store house (the church). If for no other reason, verse 11 motivates me, as I need the devourer to be rebuked for my sake. When I give the tenth, I am asking God in to cover the remaining 90 percent, and HE does.

Please do not let people tell you that giving less that ten percent is okay, or that you are tithing. If you are not giving a tenth, you are only making an offering, you are not tithing. Speaking of offering, we should give an offering to God, in addition to the tithes. Whatever the amount you and God agree upon, after the tithe (tenth) is between you and God. Whether it is $1 or $5, give it cheerfully.

It is through sharing that we bring HIS power in finances into focus. In every case, God wants us to give the first part to HIM, but HE also wants us to pay our creditors. That requires establishing a plan and probably making sacrifices of wants and desires until all obligations are current.

You cannot sacrifice God's part – that is not your option as a Christian. "Now this I say, he who sows sparingly will also reap sparingly, and he who sows bountifully will also reap bountifully" (2 Corinthians 9:6). So what is a person to do? If a sacrifice is necessary, and it almost always is, do not sacrifice God's or your creditor's share. Choose a portion of your own expenditures to sacrifice.

Save – Practice Saving

A Christian should practice saving money on a regular basis. This includes those who are in debt; especially those who are in debt. Even if it is only $5 a month, develop a discipline of saving.

This does not mean to store up a large amount of money while failing to pay your obligations, but one of the best habits you can develop is to save a small amount on a regular basis. Another thing that stood out for me in the class is the principle of saving that the Bible speaks of in the book of Proverbs regarding the ant. The verse speaks of how they store or save food during the summer so they will have food when it gets cold. This really convicted my soul. Winter or hard times will come. How are we preparing?

[6] Take a lesson from the ants, you lazybones.
   Learn from their ways and become wise!
[7] Though they have no prince
   or governor or ruler to make them work,
[8] they labor hard all summer,
   gathering food for the winter.
Proverbs 6:6-8

²⁵ Ants—they aren't strong,
   but they store up food all summer.
Proverbs 30:25

I remember the time when I did not save anything at all, how hard life was for me. When I had a flat tire, I thought my life was over; especially if I had to replace the tire. When my tags and registration expired on my car, I would drive around scared with them expired until I could get the money to take care of it. I had been driving the car all year, with the date displayed on the outside, yet, when it expired, I acted like it was a surprise. It was the same with tires, or brakes, or battery, etc, with the car. I acted like those things did not need to be replaced, or would not wear out. One thing I can say, is that when those things did happen to me, God was always on time with an answer, as it was not a surprise to HIM. I believe it was because I put HIM first with my tithe and offering.

²⁰ The wise have wealth and luxury,
   but fools spend whatever they get.
Proverbs 21:20

Here again, I learned that I was acting like a fool because I spent all I received. No plan for savings. What I allowed myself to believe is that saving a little is not worth saving at all. That is a lie from the pit of hell! Pennies still add to dollars and dollars still add up to hundreds, or even thousands of dollars.

Others believe that God frowns on a Christian saving anything. This is not true or scriptural, as Proverbs 21:20 states. The common attitude in the Bible is to save on a regular basis, and it is important that Christians develop good habits to replace bad habits. There is no alternative under God's plan for being debt free.

In September, 2011, I facilitated 2 financial freedom sessions at our Singles' Summit, at the church. In January, one of the attendees (we will call her Janice) came up to me to say that she was convicted to try just saving a little at a time. She began placing small change, and even some singles, into a large empty jar. Janice said before she knew it, the jar was full! She shared with her mother what she was doing, and her mother became her accountability partner. So when Janice would call her mother to tell her she was thinking about going shopping or planning to make some type of purchase, her mother would ask her did she really need it. Her mother would then challenge her to put what she was going to spend in the jar. Janice said now she has 2 jars filled and working on her 3rd. She said she is truly amazed at how God is working in this one area. Now Janice says she is ready for more.

Steady plodding does lead to prosperity......... Proverbs 21:5

Remember, God does have an order; Give, Save, Spend (*with a written plan*) and learn Contentment. If we tithe, but are not saving or spending with a plan, or content, we will not see God's fullness in our finances.

Spend – With a Written Plan

What do we mean by a written plan? It is a spending plan or budget, yes budget. I use to think it was a bad word, too. I thought living on a budget was restricting me from spending my money, my way, What I discovered was that it was not my money anyway, and God does have a plan for how it should be spent. It is absolutely necessary for everyone who is a steward of God's resources, especially, if you are in financial bondage. In the book of Habakkuk, chapter 2, there is a verse that speaks of writing the vision down and making it plain on the tablets. We should write down our financial vision, on paper, and make it plain.

> [1] I will climb up to my watchtower
> and stand at my guardpost.
> There I will wait to see what the LORD says
> and how he will answer my complaint.
> [2] Then the LORD said to me,
> "Write my answer plainly on tablets,
> so that a runner can carry the correct
> message to others.
> [3] This vision is for a future time.
> It describes the end, and it will be fulfilled.
> If it seems slow in coming, wait patiently,
> for it will surely take place.
> It will not be delayed.

Although, Habakkuk was speaking of a different end, we can use the same principle regarding finances. Use a written plan of all expenditures in order of their importance. The order of importance is crucial because we have lost the point of reference between needs, wants, and desires. Let's examine the differences between a need, a want, and a desire.

Needs. These are the purchases necessary to provide basic requirements, such as food, clothing, a job, shelter, medical coverage, and others. *"If we have food and covering, with these we shall be content".* (I Timothy 6:8)

Wants. Wants involve choices about the quality of goods to be used: dress clothes verses work clothes or shopping at a "low end" store verses the mall, steak versus hamburger, a new car versus a used car. These verses give a point of reference for determining wants in a Christian's life: *"Your adornment must not be merely external—braiding the hair, and wearing gold jewelry, or putting on dresses; but let it be the hidden person of the heart, with the imperishable quality of a gentle and quiet spirit, which is precious in the sight of God".* (I Peter 3:3-4)

Desires. These are choices according to God's plan that can be made only out of surplus funds after all other obligations have been met.
"Do not love the world nor the things in the world. If anyone loves the world, the love of the Father is not in him. For all that is in the world, the lust of the flesh

and the lust of the eyes and the boastful pride of life, is not from the Father, but is from the world". (I John 2:15-16)

    This was a valuable lesson for me to learn. Once I learned that I was actually putting on the external for other people, with my money, it allowed me to have a change of mind and heart. People who know me will tell you that I pretty much wear the same stuff all the time. I may add a blouse, or a jacket/blazer, some shoes, or some earrings a couple of times a year, but hardly ever a whole new outfit. I have a budget for the dry cleaners of $25 a month and save $30 a month for clothing. I may shop for clothing every 3 to 4 months. This practice has been very freeing for me. I make sure that I do not gain weight, so I can continue to wear what I have. Now, I am loosing quite a bit of weight and will have to buy some new clothes. However, I am doing it very slow and only replacing worn out shoes or a blouse here and there. I am saving the bulk of my clothing budget for my shopping spree of smaller size clothes. YEAH!

    When I am asked to speak at an event, I wear what I already have, as most of the people there don't know me well enough to know what I have in my closet.

They would not know if the outfit I had on was new or not. As long as I am clean and smell good, that is all that matters.

What are you ready to receive?
- a. God's forgiveness and financial plan for your life?
- b. Preparation for the journey – Instruction/knowledge?

⁴⁻¹⁰ *"But don't look for someone to blame.*
No finger pointing! You, priest,
are the one in the dock.
You stumble around in broad daylight, And then the prophets take over and stumble all night.
Your mother is as bad as you. My people are ruined because they don't know what's right or true.
Because you've turned your back on knowledge, I've turned my back on you priests. Because you refuse to recognize the revelation of God, I'm no longer recognizing your children.
The more priests, the more sin.
They traded in their glory for shame.
They pig out on my people's sins.

They can't wait for the latest in evil. The result: You can't tell the people from the priests,
the priests from the people.
I'm on my way to make them both pay
and take the consequences of the bad lives they've lived. They'll eat and be as hungry as ever,
have sex and get no satisfaction.
They walked out on me, their God,
for a life of rutting with whores.
Hosea 4:6-10 (MSG)

   c. Wise counsel along the way? – Proverbs 12:15 (MSG)

[15] Fools are headstrong and do what they like; wise people take advice.

Questions to Ponder:
1. Am I ready to receive God's plan, according to HIS word, or is there more to release?
2. Will I begin to trust God today and bring the whole tithe (*a tenth*) to the store house?
3. Will I begin to save regularly, even if it is a $1 a week, today?

4. Determine if I am spending in the needs, wants, or desires category and adjust accordingly.
5. Review previous bank statements (30 to 60 days) to determine current spending habits and where adjustments need to be made.
6. Find and sign up a Crown Financial Life Group at www.crown.org. Dave Ramsey's Financial Peace University at www.daveramsey.com.

5

Retain – Walk around the deep hole.

I have hidden your word in my heart,
that I might not sin against you.
Psalm 119:11

9 -16 How can a young person live a clean life?
By carefully reading the map of your Word.
I'm single-minded in pursuit of you;
don't let me miss the road signs you've posted.
I've banked your promises in the vault of my heart
so I won't sin myself bankrupt.
Be blessed, God;
train me in your ways of wise living.
I'll transfer to my lips
all the counsel that comes from your mouth;
I delight far more in what you tell me about living

> *than in gathering a pile of riches.*
> *I ponder every morsel of wisdom from you,*
> *I attentively watch how you've done it.*
> *I relish everything you've told me of life,*
> *I won't forget a word of it.*
> Psalm 119:9-16 (MSG)

AA Steps 8-11

8. Made a list of all persons we had harmed, and became willing to make amends to them all.
9. Made direct amends to such people wherever possible, except when to do so would injure them or others.
10. Continued to take personal inventory, and when we were wrong, promptly admitted it.
11. Sought through prayer and meditation to improve our conscious contact with God as we understood Him, praying only for knowledge of His will for us and the power to carry that out.

Now it is time to put into practice what we have learned so far. We have gone over a few scriptures and principles and are now ready to put it all into action – Write the financial vision down, make it plain.

If you are anything like me, there have been lots of praying and crying out to God. Asking yourself, how you could get your finances so messed up. Why you made such bad financial decisions?

It is time to put the past behind you and move forward, with Gods' help. We will cry out like David did in Psalm 102:1-3 regarding our finances.

A prayer of one overwhelmed with trouble, pouring out problems before the LORD.

[1] LORD, hear my prayer!
Listen to my plea!
[2] Don't turn away from me
in my time of distress.
Bend down to listen,
and answer me quickly when I call to you.
[3] For my days disappear like smoke,
and my bones burn like red-hot coals.

I still have to do this on a regular basis to make sure I keep my finances in line with Gods' will. There are so many distractors working to separate us from our money, and the plan God has for it. There are family members always having a crisis. There are children, grandchildren and great grandchildren, who spend all of their money because Mom or Granny will come to the rescue. There are co-workers and friends who always have some sort of crisis. There are those wicked department stores with sales. There are television, radio and internet ads drawing us away from our money. There is even the church drawing us away from our money. What I have learned, and what I will say to you is, if you did not plan for the spending activity, whatever it is, do not, I repeat, do not spend the money. Trust me, you will regret it later.

It is going to be very hard at first; however, it does gets easier with time. You learn to say, "That activity is not in my spending plan. Maybe I can next time." You do not say that you do not have the money for the activity, you just say that the activity is not part of your planned spending. As you continue to practice this discipline, you will see amazing results, as well as be a witness to your friends, family, co-workers, etc. They will begin to see the fruit of your labor and ask you to help them.

Let's now look at the steps to making a spending plan. As we look at the steps, please keep in mind that no two budgets are exactly alike. They may have some of the same components, but they will not be exactly alike.

In making and using a budget or spending plan, there are several logical steps, each requiring individual effort. You can find printable forms online at www.crown.org. You can print as many as you need from the website. Use these forms to guide your budget preparation.

Before we proceed, if you did not do so in chapter 4, please take the time to review your bank statements to get an idea of where your money is going. This is the pre-work to following the steps that are to follow.

Step 1 – List Monthly Expenditures in the Home.
   a. Fixed Expenses
      Tithe (*10%*)
      Federal income taxes (*if taxes are deducted from your check ignore this item*)
      Federal Social Security taxes (*if taxes are deducted from your check, ignore this item*)
      Housing expenses (*mortgage/rent*)

Property taxes

Property insurance (*home owners or rental*)

Other (*anything else you spend to keep your home, such as, alarm system, cable/internet, telephone (land line or cell, maintenance and yard care*)

b. Variable Expenses

Food

Outstanding debts

Utilities

Insurance (life, health, auto premiums only)

Entertainment, recreation

Clothing allowance

Medical/dental (your out of pocket Dr. visits and prescriptions)

Savings

Miscellaneous

NOTE: In order to accurately determine variable expenses, if married, it is suggested that both husband and wife keep an expense diary for 30 days. Every expenditure, no matter how small, should be listed. Yes, that means vending machines, convenience store drive bys, etc.

Please listen to me carefully; Step 1 will not work if you do not review previous bank statements to see how your money is being spent. It also gives a financial picture of what is important to you, or "where your heart is".

Step 2 – List Available Monthly Income

NOTE: If you operate on a non-fixed income, use a yearly average divided into months.

Salary	Interest
Rents	Dividends
Notes	Income Tax Refunds
Other	

Step 3 – Compare Income verses Expenses

Couples are strongly encouraged to establish a budget on the husband's income only. It is recommended that the wife's income be applied to one-time purchases only—vacations, furniture, cars—or to savings or debt reduction. Too many times the wife's income is interrupted by illness, pregnancy, or a change in the husband's employment location.

If total income exceeds total expenses, you only have to implement a method of budget control in your home. However, if your expenses exceed your income (or more stringent controls in spending are desired), additional steps are necessary. In that case, to reduce expenses, an analysis in each budget area is called for. These areas are outlined below.

"Budget Busters" are the largest potential problem areas that can ruin a budget. Budget busters are the housing, food and automobile categories. Failure to control even one of these problems can result in financial disaster in the home. This area is evaluated by typical budget percentages for a $35,000 annual income (family of four). Naturally, these percentages are not absolutes and will vary with income and geographical location. For more information on budget busters, please visit www.crown.org, online articles, budgeting.

Crown Financial uses a 14 point Monthly Income and Expenses sheet or budget sheet. You can download from their free online tools section at www.crown.org. Categories one and two are the Tithe and Taxes, which are subtracted from your Gross Monthly Income to get your Net Spendable Income, or NSI. This is what categories 3 through 14 are subtracted from.

3 **Housing (36 percent of net income)**
   Typically, this is one of the largest home budget problems. Many families, motivated by peer pressure or some other pressure, buy homes they can't afford. It is not necessary for everyone to own a home. The decision to buy or rent should be based on needs and financial ability, rather than on internal or external pressure.

My journey to home ownership was long. I purchased by first home when I was married, in 1980. Neither us knew the Lord at the time. Our home was not built on the solid foundation of Christ, and crumbled pretty fast. After my divorce, we lived in many apartments and townhomes. The journey to home ownership did not really begin until 2005, when I surrendered my financial life over to God. I accepted Christ in 1984, but did not surrender my financial life over until the Fall of 2005. Prior to that, I gave into the peer pressure of home ownership. Family members, co-workers, as well as church members would constantly tell me that I should be in a home. They would remind me that I had a great job with great income and therefore, I should be in a home.

Right before I discovered the class, there was a home that I spotted and wanted to purchase. I sought no wise counsel, or even asked God. I just believed it was my time. So, I met with owners and struck up a deal. I could feel the Holy Spirit telling me that it was not time, but I continued to move forward. Right after I signed the contract and gave them $1700 earnest money, I was convicted. This was not my house, and this was not my time. I immediately contacted the couple and shared with them what the Lord had shared with me. Of course, they tried to talk me into moving forward, as they reminded me that I would not get my earnest money back. I thanked them for their time and told them this was a $1700 lesson that I will never forget. From then on, I was content in apartment living, until God decided differently, not me.

As stated earlier, we moved out of the townhome we were living in and moved to the Budget Suites of America. We lived there from 2005 to 2007. During this time, I worked on my budget as I prepared for apartment living. In April of 2007, the Lord said it was time to look for an apartment. How did I know it was the Lord? For me it was going about my normal routine and suddenly, I begin to notice the apartment neighborhoods I was driving by. Before, I did not even notice them. I settled on an apartment and planned for the August move. This was also the year I paid off my SUV and became debt free! I continued to work my budget and laid out a five year plan for home ownership.

Of course, there was a setback in the journey. In 2008, shortly after I was celebrating being debt free, my daughter, who was in the 11th grade at time, became pregnant, and in November of 2008, my beautiful grandson, Jaden, was born. Of course, this was not in the budget. However, God is the only one that gives life, and this was her time. As a minor, she was still on my medical insurance, so this would have to be taken care of. As a mother, I was very upset, but deep down inside, knew that God would provide, and he did. We utilized the services of the Family Care Pregnancy Center through our church, and it was truly a blessing! The classes and support they provided were truly a God send. They even give the girls that go through the program a baby shower. Needless to say, it took a while to get back on track, but with much prayer, discipline and perseverance, I did get back on track.

In 2010, I began to look online, as well as ask around, for free home ownership classes in the community. I attended a few, but then, while sitting in church one Sunday, I read in the bulletin that my church was putting on a home buyers' class, through the outreach arm of the church. Of course I attended and received some information that led me to D.R. Horton's FREE Home Buying Club, DHI Home Buying Club. This was September, 2010. I immediately looked them up online and completed their intake application. Thus, the journey to home ownership continues. I had 2 years left in my 5 year plan and was very excited!

I continued to work on my budget, and followed the instruction of my DHI case worker, as I reminded my now adult children that they were not in it. My daughter was now working and living on her own, as she is not a good roommate. In September, 2011, the case worker sent me an email saying I was pre-approved, and ready to pick out my home. This was very exciting, especially since my lease would be up in November.

I do want to share with you that the amount I was approved for was over my budgeted amount, but it was very tempting. I did go over to one of the new D.R. Horton areas and pick out a home. However, right in the middle of speaking with the realtor, I was convicted and shared with her that these homes are not in my budget. I then began to look for homes within my budget of $100, 000 or less. Whenever I would find one I liked, it was instantly purchased. My DHI case worker suggested that I get a realtor, and she recommended a great one. She is a Pastor's wife and an anointed woman of God. I told her what I was looking for, and my dream home was in the first 4 homes she showed me. They were all brand new homes, in a new neighborhood. I put down the earnest money and we were on our way. The entire process took less than 30 days. WOW!

I was moving into my dream home, within my budget. My 3-bedroom, 2 full bath, 2 car garage, home is only $63 more dollars than my 2-bedrooom, 2 full bath, no garage apartment. God is so good! My son still lives with me, but he is moving into his own place soon. I shared this with you as I want you to know that if you wait on God, He will come through. Please know that your wait may not be the same as my wait; but if you follow the principles in this book, you will see the fruit of your labor.

NOTE: Please don't pay 12 months for extra rooms in your home or apartment that will only be occupied once or twice a year. When family or others come to visit, I am sure they would not mind temporarily sleeping on the couch, or on an air mattress. That is what my sister does when she comes to visit. She actually prefers the couch, even though my son offers up his room to her. Now if your guest has a medical condition or their age will not allow them to sleep on the couch or air mattress, then give up your room and you sleep on the couch or the air mattress. It is only temporary, and the purpose of the visit is fellowship.

4   **Food (12 percent of net income)**

   Many families buy too much food. Others buy too little. Typically, the average American family buys the wrong type of food. The reduction of a family's food bill requires quantity and quality planning.

Hints for Grocery Shopping

- Always use a written list of needs.
- Try to conserve gas by buying food for a longer time period and in larger quantities.
- Avoid buying when hungry (especially if you're a "sugarholic").
- Use a calculator, if possible, to total purchases.

- Reduce or eliminate paper products—paper plates, cups, napkins (use cloth napkins).
- Evaluate where to purchase sundry items, such as shampoo, mouthwash. (These are normally somewhat cheaper at discount stores.)
- Avoid processed and sugar-coated cereals. (These are expensive and most of them have little nutritional value.)
- Avoid prepared foods, such as frozen dinners, pot pies, cakes. (You are paying for expensive labor that you can provide.)
- Determine good meat cuts that are available from roasts or shoulders, and have the butcher cut these for you. (Buying steaks by the package on sale is fairly inexpensive also.)
- Try store brand canned products. (These are normally cheaper and just as nutritious.)
- Avoid products in a seasonal price hike. Substitute or eliminate.
- Shop for advertised specials. (These are usually posted in the store window.)
- Use manufacturer's coupons (cents-off on an item or items) only if you were going to buy the item anyway and it is cheaper than another brand would be without the coupon.

- When possible, purchase food in bulk quantities from large discount stores; the per-item cost is cheaper. Do not buy from convenience stores except in case of emergency.
- Avoid buying non-grocery items in a grocery supermarket except on sale. (These are normally "high mark-up" items.)
- For baby foods, use normal foods processed in a blender.
- Leave the children at home to avoid unnecessary pressure.
- Check every item as it is being "rung up" at the store and again when you get home.
- Consider canning fresh vegetables whenever possible. Make bulk purchases with other families at farmers' markets and such. (NOTE: Secure canning supplies during off seasons.)

5 Automobiles (12 percent of net income)

The advertising media refers to us as "consumers," but that's not always the best description. P.T. Barnum had a more apt word—"suckers." Often we are unwise in our decision making when it comes to our machines—especially cars.

Many families will buy new cars they cannot afford and trade them long before their utility is depleted. Those who buy a new car, keep it for less than four years, and then trade it for a new model have wasted the maximum amount of money. Some people, such as salespeople who drive a great deal, need new cars frequently; most of us do not. We swap cars because we want to—not because we have to. Many factors enter here, such as ego, esteem, and maturity. You can live without a car note. My vehicle is 10 years old this year and still going strong. People regularly ask me about getting a new car. I polite tell them if they are going to pay the note, I will drive the car.

6 Insurance (5 percent of net income)

It is unfortunate to see so many families misled in this area. Few people understand insurance, either how much is needed or what kind is necessary. Who would be foolish enough to buy a Rolls Royce when he or she could afford only a Chevrolet? Yet many purchase high-cost insurance even though their needs dictate otherwise.

Insurance should be used as supplementary provision for the family, not for protection or profit. An insurance plan is not designed for saving money or for retirement. Ask anyone who assumed it was; the ultimate result was disillusionment and disappointment.

In our society, insurance can be used as an inexpensive vehicle to provide future family income and thus release funds today for family use and the Lord's work. In excess, this same insurance can put a family in debt, steal the Lord's money, and transfer dependence to the world.

One of your best insurance assets is to have a trustworthy agent in charge of your program. A good insurance agent is usually one who can select from several different companies to provide you with the best possible buy and who will create a brief, uncomplicated plan to analyze your exact needs.

7   Debts (5 percent of net income)

It would be great if most budgets included 5 percent debts or less. Unfortunately, the norm in American families is far in excess of this amount. As previously discussed, credit cards, bank loans, and installment credit have made it possible for families to go deeply into debt. What things can you do once this situation exists?

- Destroy all credit cards as a first step.
- Establish a payment schedule that includes all creditors.
- Contact all creditors, honestly relate your problems, and arrange an equitable repayment plan.
- Buy on a cash basis, and sacrifice your wants and desires until you are current.

8 Entertainment/Recreation (6 percent of net income)

We are a recreation-oriented country. That is not necessarily bad if put in the proper perspective. But those who are in debt cannot use their creditor's money to entertain themselves. The normal tendency is to escape problems, even if only for a short while—even if the problems then become more acute. Christians must resist this urge and control recreation and entertainment expenses while in debt.

What a terrible witness it is for a Christian who is already in financial bondage to indulge at the expense of others. God knows we need rest and relaxation, and once our attitude is correct He will often provide it from unexpected sources. Every believer, whether in debt or not, should seek to reduce entertainment expenses. This usually can be done without sacrificing quality family time.

Recreation Hints

- Plan vacations during "off seasons" if possible.
- Consider a camping vacation to avoid motel and food expenses. (Christian friends can pool the expenses of camping items.)
- Select vacation areas in your general locale.
- Use some family games in place of movies (like some of those unused games received at Christmas).
- To reduce expenses and increase fellowship, consider taking vacation trips with two or more families.
- If flying, use the least expensive coach fare (i.e., late night or early morning usually saves 10 percent to 20 percent).
- Eating out falls under this category. Please monitor this closely. Many families have fallen prey to the "eating out syndrome". There is nothing wrong with eating out, if it is a planned expense. No one knows your schedule like you. Plan on eating out with those activities that are keeping

you away from home, like school and church activities. Determine a reasonable, set amount that you and your family can commit to for eating out and stick to it.
- Paying for Baby Sitters, outside of normal day-care expenses
- Add church to this category. If you purchase sermons, books, etc from your church, add them to this category.

9 Clothing (5 percent of net income)

Many families in debt sacrifice this area in their budget because of excesses in other areas. And yet with prudent planning and buying your family can be clothed neatly without great expense. This requires effort on your part in terms of:

1. Saving enough money to buy without using credit.
2. Educating family members on care of clothing.
3. Applying discipline with children to enforce these habits.
4. Developing skills in making and mending clothing.

Learn to be utilizers of resources rather than consumers. How many families have closets full of clothes they no longer wear because they are "out of style"?

Many families with large surplus incomes spend excessively in the area of clothes.

Assess whether it really matters that you have all of the latest styles. Do your purchases reflect good utility rather than ego? Do you buy clothes to satisfy a need or a desire?

Budget Hints

- Make as many of the clothes as time will allow. (Average savings is 50 percent to 60 percent.)
- Make a written list of clothing needs and purchase during the "off" season when possible.
- Select outfits that can be mixed and used in multiple combinations rather than as a single set.
- Frequent the discount outlets that carry unmarked name-brand goods.
- Shop at authentic factory outlet stores for close-out values of top quality.
- Select clothing made of home washable fabrics.
- Use coin-operated dry cleaning machines instead of commercial cleaners.

- Practice early repair for damaged clothing.
- Learn to utilize all clothing fully (especially children's wear).

10 Savings (5 percent of net income)

It is important that some savings be established in the budget. Otherwise, the use of credit becomes a lifelong necessity and debt a way of life. Your savings will allow you to purchase items for cash and shop for the best buys, irrespective of the store.

Savings Hints

- Use a company payroll withdrawal, if possible. This removes the money before you receive it.
- Use an automatic bank withdrawal from your checking account.
- Write your savings account a check just as if it were a creditor.
- When an existing debt is paid off, allocate any extra money toward the next largest debt. When all consumer debt is paid off, then reallocate that money to savings.

- My church has a credit union. It really helps me to save, as it is not that easy to get to the money. If your church as a credit union, try it.

11 Medical/dental expenses (4 percent of net income)

You must anticipate these expenses in your budget and set aside funds regularly; failure to do so will wreck your plans and lead to indebtedness. Do not sacrifice family health due to lack of planning; but, at the same time, do not use doctors excessively. Proper prevention is much cheaper than correction.

You can avoid many dental bills by teaching children to eat the right foods and clean their teeth properly. Your dentist can supply all the information you need on this subject.

Many doctor bills can be avoided in the same way. Take proper care of your body through diet, rest, and exercise, and it will respond with good health. Abuse your body and you must ultimately pay through illnesses and malfunctions. This is not to say that all illnesses or problems are caused by neglect, but a great many are.

Do not be hesitant to question doctors and dentists in advance about costs. Also, educate yourself enough to discern when you are getting good value for your money. Most ethical professionals will not take offense at your questions. If they do, that may be a hint to change services.

In the case of prescriptions, shop around. You will be amazed to discover the wide variance in prices from one store to the next. Ask about generic drugs. These are usually much less expensive and are just as effective.

12 Miscellaneous (variable expenses) (5 percent of net income)

These can include a myriad of items. Some of the expenses occur monthly and others occur on an as-needed basis (such as appliances).

One of the most important factors in home expenses is you. If you can perform routine maintenance and repair, considerable expenses can be avoided. Many people rationalize not doing these things on the basis that time is too valuable. That is nonsense. If every hour of the day is tied up in the pursuit of money, as previously defined, then you're in bondage.

A part of care and maintenance around the home relates to family life, particularly the training of children. When they see mom and dad willing to do some physical labor to help around the home, they will learn good habits. But if you refuse to get involved, why should they? Where will they ever learn the skills of self-sufficiency?

Some men avoid working on home projects because they say they lack the necessary skills. Well, those skills are learned, not gifted. There are many good books that detail every area of home maintenance. As previously mentioned, at some point in the future many of these skills will be necessities rather than choices.

Some items that could be included in this category are: toiletry/ cosmetic, beauty/barber, laundry/ cleaning, allowances/lunches, subscriptions, gifts (includes Christmas), Cash, Internet (this could be under housing as well), Other (this is where I have my grandson-not my children).

13 Investments (5 percent of net income)

Individuals and families with surplus income in their budgets will have the opportunity to invest for retirement or other long-term goals. As debt-free status is achieved, more money can be diverted to this category.

14 School/Child Care (6 percent of net income) (If this category is used, other categories must be adjusted downward a total of 6 percent.)

An ever increasing segment of our population has expenses for private school and/or child care. This category must reflect those expenses. All other categories must be reduced to provide these funds.

Some items that can be included in this category are: Tuition, materials, transportation, Day Care, other.

Unallocated Surplus Income

Income from unallocated sources (garage sales, gifts) can be kept in one's checking account and placed in this category. This category is also useful for recording income information for tax purposes.

Variable Income Planning

Families with variable monthly incomes need budgets even more than families on fixed salaries. Many people with fluctuating incomes get trapped into debt because they borrow during lean months and spend what they make during high-income months, rather than repaying what they previously borrowed.

Proverbs 27:12 says, *"A prudent man sees evil and hides himself, the naive proceed and pay the penalty."*

Living on a fluctuating income can be very deceiving—and difficult. Months of high income can easily be construed as a windfall profit. To properly budget a variable income you must conservatively estimate what your annual income is likely to be, divide that by 12, and then develop your monthly budget based on that amount. You should put all your income into a savings account and withdraw your average monthly salary from that account each month.

This method will allow surplus funds from higher income months to accumulate in the savings account to cover budgeted expenses during months of lower income. This is not hoarding; it is planning according to Proverbs 6:6-8.

Questions to Ponder:
1. Am I really ready to begin the journey to true financial freedom?
2. Do I know where my money is going? Proverbs 27:23 say, "²³ Know the state of your flocks, and put your heart into caring for your herds,....."
3. Do I have more income than expenditures? If so, how will I manage the surplus?

4. Do I have more expenditures than income? If so, what drastic measures will I take to reduce the expenditures?
5. After looking at your income and expenses, what adjustments do you need to make?
6. Are you ready and willing to make those adjustments?
7. Prayerfully and diligently work through your budget.

6

Rejoice – As you walk down another street, with the Lord.

Chapter V
I walk down another street.

> [4] *Always be full of joy in the Lord.*
> *I say it again—rejoice!*
> Philippians 4:4

AA Step 12

> *12. Having had a spiritual awakening as the result of these steps, we tried to carry this message and to practice these principles in all our affairs.*

There are many reasons to rejoice as God moves through your finances and you see and experience the fruit of your labor. As you experience financial freedom with God, you will find your own way of rejoicing. Below are just a few that I personally experienced.

Stop Borrowing – Do not take on any new debt. I did take out a loan for my new home, as God did not provide the funds for me to pay cash. However, opening up a bunch of new consumer debt has not taken control of me. Now, the urge does come over me now and then, but I do not act on it. It is such a wonderful feeling to submit those desires to God, as I know that on my own, I am not strong enough to resist.

Debt slowly disappears *(remember, steady plodding brings prosperity)* – Focus on and pay off one debt at a time. It took a while to get into this situation, so we have to allow some time to get out of it. It is like shedding off weight, we can only do it one pound at a time.

Money is freed up – It is so nice to have money to do things for the Kingdom of God and not be stressed out or worried after doing it. Remember, if you serve in a ministry in your church or outside of church, the cost of that activity should be reflected in your budget as a planned expense. You know what type of financial needs the ministry has that you are serving in, it should not be a surprise or derail your budget when a donation is asked for. An example is that I serve in two ministries at my church, the Greeters ministry and the Stewardship Ministry. In the Greeters' ministry, twice a year, I have to contribute towards food for the monthly meeting. I have that in my food budget. Also, in the Stewardship ministry, we take turns bringing the "nugget" to the meeting, and the "nugget" person is also responsible for bringing breakfast. I have that expense in with my food budget as well. It is so nice not to be stressed out about when that time comes.

Freedom to make choices about spending – I am free to make choices about where my money goes, instead of it telling me where to go. I do not feel the pressure from my peers or society about how I manage the resources God has entrusted me with. I do not feel the need to apologize. I am very much content.

Share principles with others – For me, this is one of the best parts. God has allowed to share at my church by facilitating other classes, as well as one on one budget coaching. The Director of our Couples' Ministry, as well as the Director of our Counseling Ministry send couples and singles to me for budget coaching who are having trouble with their finances. I asked them why one day, and they both told me it is because after working with me the past few years, they know that I am only going to share with them the word of God, and not my opinion. It was very humbling and encouraging for me to hear.

I have also been asked to speak on financial freedom at local churches and across the nation. It has truly been a blessing to me to share what God has taught me about finances and managing His money. Now there are those folks out there who do not want to hear this message, either because it is not their time, or they have bought into the world's view that if you do not live in a mansion or drive a certain type of car, that you are not equipped to tell them about finances. I am so glad that God knows where the people are who want to hear from Him.

It's almost funny! I think about how the Bible describes John the Baptist. If he were around today, I wonder how many people would receive his message and allow him to baptized them. It is the word that people should be focusing on and not the messenger. Matthew 6:30-33 tells us, *[30-33]"If God gives such attention to the appearance of wildflowers—most of which are never even seen—don't you think he'll attend to you, take pride in you, do his best for you? What I'm trying to do here is to get you to relax, to not be so preoccupied with getting, so you can respond to God's giving. People who don't know God and the way he works fuss over these things, but you know both God and how he works. Steep your life in God-reality, God-initiative, God-provisions. Don't worry about missing out. You'll find all your everyday human concerns will be met.* (MSG)

Seek a lifestyle of obedience – staying on the vine and bearing fruit – much fruit.

[5] "Yes, I am the vine; you are the branches. Those who remain in me, and I in them, will produce much fruit. For apart from me you can do nothing. [6] Anyone who does not remain in me is thrown away like a useless branch and withers. Such branches are gathered into a pile to be burned. [7] But if you remain in me and my words remain in you, you may ask for anything

you want, and it will be granted! ⁸ *When you produce much fruit, you are my true disciples. This brings great glory to my Father.*

⁹ *"I have loved you even as the Father has loved me. Remain in my love.* ¹⁰ *When you obey my commandments, you remain in my love, just as I obey my Father's commandments and remain in his love.* ¹¹ *I have told you these things so that you will be filled with my joy. Yes, your joy will overflow!* John 15:5-11

⁴⁶⁻⁴⁷*"Why are you so polite with me, always saying 'Yes, sir,' and 'That's right, sir,' but never doing a thing I tell you? These words I speak to you are not mere additions to your life, homeowner improvements to your standard of living. They are foundation words, words to build a life on.* Luke 6:46-47

It's your decision today: Whom will you serve?

For further reading:
Deuteronomy 28:1-2; 12-13; 15, 43-44
Joshua 24:14-15
Luke 16:13

7

Revisit/Review

*⁵ Good planning and hard work lead to prosperity,
but hasty shortcuts lead to poverty.*
Proverbs 21:5

Just like you cannot go on a diet for one week or a month and reach your desired weight goal, you cannot look at your finances for a week or a month and reach your financial goal. You are going to have to revisit and review them often. I tell my coaching clients that you have to keep your budget with you at all times, and have copies available in your home where you spend time, especially in the bathroom. Yes, I said the bathroom. The bathroom is a great place to work on your budget. It is generally quiet in there, with minimal activity going on. You will find that if you spend 15 minutes a week on your budget, you will have a good idea of where your money is going and where adjustments need to be made.

You will also need to find YOUR preferred method of budgeting. There are so many tools out there; you will have to spend time exploring which one works best for you. For me, I have found that the old fashion pencil and paper work best for me. I have a tablet that I strictly use for budgeting. I also found that the envelope system works best for me for my variable expenses. If I know I am going to the grocery store, I take out the cash that is allocated for groceries and take it with me, instead of my debit card. I learned in the class that up to 27% more is spent using a card verses cash. I realized this is true because even though I had a list, I would add a few more items that I did not budget for to the basket, because I knew I could put it on the card. I have learned to budget for a few extra items so I am not going over my budget when I take the cash with me. I also use the calculator on my cell phone to make sure I am on target.

In addition to reviewing your budget weekly, you need to review your debts monthly, or quarterly. If someone walked up to you and told you that they were going to pay off all your debts, would you be able to give them an exact amount? You should always know the state of your financial affairs. Do not hide from your debts, run to them. With God running ahead of you, you will be able to pay them off, even student loans. Yes, student loans! One of the young ladies that serve in the Stewardship ministry with me paid off $15,000 in student loan debt in 18 months. Unbelievable? Not with God! With God, ALL things are possible, if you just believe. Steading plodding. Consider the ant. Proverbs 6:6-8

You must also revisit and review your surroundings. Who are you spending time with? Are they a help or hindrance? Do they push you toward God and HIS financial goal for your life, or are they pulling you away from your target? What do you listen to in your car? Is it information that is pointing you toward your financial goal? I listen to 90.9 KCBI, as they air much teaching, as well as wonderful worship music. I also listen to them because my pastor comes on weekdays at 11:30am, Central Standard Time. You can also listen to them on the internet, as well as download their app. They have prayer every half hour that is very encouraging. Dave Ramsey is also on the radio, several stations actually. Look him up to see where you can pick him up. You have got to revisit and review what is going in your soul. Like my parents and grandparents use to say, "What goes in is what will come out."

What do you watch on television? There are some great financial shows on the air these days. Suzy Orman comes on MSNBC regularly. Look her up. She has some great financial advice on her show. There is another show that I also discovered on MSNBC called, "Till Debt Do Us Part". It comes on Saturday nights. Look it up. It has some great financial tips for managing your money and getting out of debt. Remember, we must make some drastic changes regarding our finances if we want to see some drastic results. Do I need to remind you again the definition of insanity? Doing the same thing over and over again and expecting different results.

Questions to Ponder:
1. How often will you review your budget?
2. How often will you review your debt? When is "D" day (debt free day)
3. What changes have you decided to make regarding your intake – radio, television, conversation?
4. Are you insane?

8

A Suitable Helper

¹⁸ Then the LORD God said, "It is not good for the man to be alone. I will make a helper who is just right for him."
Genesis 2:18

A Wife of Noble Character
¹⁰ Who can find a virtuous and capable wife? She is more precious than rubies. ¹¹ Her husband can trust her, and she will greatly enrich his life. ¹² She brings him good, not harm, all the days of her life. Proverbs 31:10-12

…………..and the wife must respect her husband.
Ephesians 5:33

I am sure you are thinking, what does all the previous information have to do with being a wife. Maybe you are single and have no interest in getting married. Maybe you have been married for a long time and feel like things are just going to be the way they are. It is too late for change. Well, let me start off by saying, whether you are single and content, single and want to be married, newly married, or married for a long time, this information is still for you. We all need to know how to manage our finances to the glory of God.

Wherever your treasure is, there the desires of your heart will also be.
Matthew 6:21, Luke 12:34

Single Ladies, if you do not want to be married, then the Lord is your husband and you still need to learn how to manage YOUR finances in a way that brings HIM glory. If you want to be married, are you a Suitable Helper for him? Remember, the Bibles states a man that finds a wife finds a good thing and receives favor from God, not finds a Single woman.

> ²² *The man who finds a wife finds a treasure,*
> *and he receives favor from the LORD.*
> Proverbs 18:22

Can a man trust you with the finances? Will you greatly enrich his life? Will you bring him good and not harm, ALL the days of your life? Think about it. If you are Single and want to be married, how are you preparing for that season in your life? What are you doing, right now, that is getting your ready for the husband that you say you want? Have you read ALL the scriptures that the Bible has on marriage and family? Do you know what your role is, and what his role should be? Read Ephesians 5:22-29.

I ask these questions because I was married for 15 years, and did not have a clue on what I was doing. As mentioned earlier, my mother and grandmother were both divorced. So, I did not have marriage modeled for me. I was also not a Christian when I got married and had no idea that God ordained and had a plan for marriage. When I went through my seven year separation, and subsequent divorce, God had me read everything the Bible had to say on marriage and divorce – Old and New Testament. He would also send me to the Christian bookstore to find books that were written on marriage.

And yes, with all that reading, I still went through divorce. However, I learned a few things during that time. I learned that I could only control me and not my husband. I learned that I was out of order and needed to line up under the authority of God and my husband. I have learned that two out of order people leave no room for God to come in and dwell, as rebellion does not invite God in. I learned that it is what the word of God says that matters in the marriage, not the opinion of man or the world.

I must share that one of the books God led me to read was about the book of Hosea. I read how God sent Hosea to marry Gomer, a whore. Gomer kept running off and the Lord would have Hosea to go and bring her back, every time. I asked God at the time, why did He have me read that book, as I was not a whore. However, my husband was the one that kept running off. At the time, it never occurred to me that I needed to go and get him and bring him back, as I knew he would just wonder off again. But since I have been writing this book, I now believe that maybe, just maybe, that is what He was trying to convey over to me. I have since confessed to God and asked for forgiveness, if I did miss Him at that time. I believe it is never too late for God.

Married Ladies – Let me ask you; are you a Suitable Helper for your husband? Are you just right for him? Can your husband trust you with the finances? Are you deceitful when it comes to the finances? Are you spending money that he does not know about? Are you giving money to your children, parents or other family members that he is not aware of? Are you living like roommates with benefits, as it relates to the finances? Is ALL of your money separate? Do you go shopping for clothes, shoes or household items and hide them in the trunk of the car, the closet, and the garage or even at a friend's house? If so, STOP IT! I know it is happening as I hear about it every day. At work, at church, and especially with my budget coaching clients. Ladies, we have conformed to the world's way of doing marriage, and that is not of God. We have got to release our old way of doing marriage and finance, and embrace God's way through His word. We have got to stop focusing on what we think our husbands are not doing and focus on how we should be glorifying God by the way we treat our husbands. Is our goal to bring our husband good and not harm, ALL the days of our life? Take some time, right now, to assess your treatment of your husband. If you need to repent of some things, write them down and bring them to God, right now. Confess to God and your husband what you have discovered about yourself, and receive forgiveness. If you believe that God is not at the center of your marriage, it is time to take charge, line up under the authority of God and your husband and watch HIM move in your marriage.

It will help you get a handle on managing you as you manage God's resources if you learn as much about yourself as possible. Learn your personality type. Discover how you are wired in the natural and ask God to bring those natural tendencies under the subjection of the Holy Spirit, and He will. Believe it or not, your personality has a lot to do with your decisions around money. I learned that I am spontaneous and a free spirit in the natural; however, that behavior can be very costly, if not controlled by the Holy Spirit.

Also, if you learned what your spirit gift(s) are and what love means to you and the people you closely interact with, it will bring you focus and strengthen your relationships, as your spending habits are managed.

Ladies, it's time to walk down another street.

There are many books and resources that have helped me on this journey of being a wife. You see, I still believe I am a wife waiting to be found by my husband, my KING. See partial list below. You will find a full list in the Resource section of the book.

Resource Page

Websites:

www.crown.org> Resources> Personal> Tools/Downloads

www.crown.org>Resources>Articles>Personal

www.crown.org – Life Group

www.daveramsey.com – Financial Peace University

www.suzyorman.com

www.tonyevans.org

www.ocbfchurch.org

www.leejenkinsministries.org

www.mydfree.org

Books:

The Ryrie Study Bible

The Spirit Controlled Woman by Beverly LaHaye

Experiencing God by Henry Blackaby

Marriage Matters by Tony Evans (My Pastor)

The Role of the Woman by Tony Evans

The Role of the Man by Tony Evans
Divorce and Remarriage by Tony Evans
Kingdom Man by Tony Evans (*Every Man's Destiny. Every Woman's Dream*)

FREE Online Resources:
Personality tests
Five Love Languages quiz by Gary Smalley
Spiritual Gift Assessment

www.ingramcontent.com/pod-product-compliance
Lightning Source LLC
LaVergne TN
LVHW041711060526
838201LV00043B/675